Cakes

from the Tooth Fairy

Sue Simkins

Cakes
from the Tooth Fairy

How to bake delicious treats
that are kinder to your teeth!

SPRING HILL

Published by Spring Hill, an imprint of How To Books Ltd.
Spring Hill House, Spring Hill Road
Begbroke, Oxford OX5 1RX
United Kingdom
Tel: (01865) 375794.
Fax: (01865) 379162
info@howtobooks.co.uk
www.howtobooks.co.uk

First published 2011

How To Books greatly reduce the carbon footprint of their books by sourcing their typesetting and printing in the UK.

British Library Cataloguing in Publication Data
A catalogue record for this book is available from the British Library

ISBN: 978 1 905862 65 8

Produced for How To Books by Deer Park Productions, Tavistock, Devon
Typeset by PDQ Typesetting Ltd, Newcastle-under-Lyme, Staffordshire
Printed and bound in Great Britain by Bell & Bain Ltd, Glasgow

NOTE: The material contained in this book is set out in good faith for general guidance and no liability can be accepted for loss or expense incurred as a result of relying in particular circumstances on statements made in the book. Laws and regulations are complex and liable to change, and readers should check the current position with the relevant authorities before making personal arrangements.

Contents

Acknowledgements

I would like to thank my family and friends and everyone who has helped with the making of this book.

Special thanks to Murray Hawkins and everyone at the Winning Smiles dental practice and to Gary Rhodes and Melissa Syers.

Thank you, too, to Michael Rose.

As ever, thank you to Fanny Charles and everyone at the *Blackmore Vale Magazine*.

And, finally, a huge thank you to everyone at How To Books.

Thank you all very much indeed.

Foreword

Reading this book inspired in me a hunger to cook and nibble amongst the many sweet fancies presented. It is even more of a pleasure to read how xylitol creates a sweet bite we can all enjoy, without having to fear the damage normally done to our teeth through over-indulging in sugary delights.

I love the mix of fruity flavours, not forgetting the many British classics, which all help to inspire the mixing, whisking, baking, and – of course, the best bit – the eating.

Gary Rhodes

Introduction

This delightful little book contains delicious recipes combined with really practical tooth care advice. The recipes contain xylitol rather than sucrose or standard table sugar. Xylitol is a naturally occurring sweetener derived from wood or maize. It has been shown to confer significant oral health benefits. Whereas sucrose consumption leads to tooth decay, xylitol actively inhibits it. It encourages the remineralisation of teeth and inhibits *streptococcus mutans*, the acid-producing bacteria chiefly responsible for dental caries.

Xylitol contains about 40% less energy than sucrose and is absorbed from the gut more slowly. It is therefore of benefit to both dieters and sufferers of diabetes. There is also encouraging research to suggest that it may increase the activity of neutrophils – the white blood cells which fight bacterial infections and may also be helpful in the control of oral thrush and osteoporosis.

Cakes from the Tooth Fairy is both entertaining and informative.
I heartily recommend it to anyone serious about ensuring that their children grow up with healthy teeth – or indeed to anyone who just likes cakes!

Murray Hawkins BDS, DGPRCS (UK)

What is Xylitol?

Xylitol is a naturally occurring form of sugar (strictly speaking, it is a 'sugar alcohol'), sometimes called birch sugar. It's found in certain fruits and plants such as oats, berries, maize and birch bark. It can be extracted from some of them: usually from maize husks or birch bark. Xylitol contains the same level of sweetness as regular sugar or sucrose but with approximately 40% fewer calories and 75% fewer available carbohydrates.

Xylitol has a low impact on blood sugar and very low glycaemic index (7 or 8, compared with sucrose, which is around 65, although studies vary). Xylitol is cariostatic, which means it doesn't cause tooth decay (dental caries) and can actually help guard against it. Xylitol encourages the growth of good bacteria in the gut and discourages the growth of yeast.

Xylitol was first discovered in the 1890s and was developed further several decades later in Europe as a safer sweetener than sugar for people with diabetes. Scientists in Finland found it was a useful alternative to beet sugar during the sugar shortages of the Second World War.

It became popular in Finland and by the 1970s Finnish scientists had discovered xylitol's dental benefits.

The many health benefits of xylitol are widely documented. However, it can cause mild diarrhoea in some people if taken to excess, particularly if your body isn't used to it. Stick to a normal serving of cake – a modest slice or two, or one or two individual cakes at a sitting – and you should be fine. Possibly, if you were to eat an entire large cake all at once, you would experience some discomfort, but then again, it wouldn't be wise to eat that amount of cake made with regular sugar either! Just be sensible and take it steadily, particularly while your digestive system adapts to it.

Warning for Pets

Although beneficial for humans, xylitol – much like chocolate and grapes – **is not suitable for dogs**. In fact, it is not advisable to give it to any animal, so please keep anything made with xylitol, and xylitol itself, for human consumption only. If you suspect your dog has taken xylitol, please consult your vet immediately.

Oven Temperature Conversions

Mark 1	275°F	140°C
Mark 2	300°F	150°C
Mark 3	325°F	170°C
Mark 4	350°F	180°C
Mark 5	375°F	190°C
Mark 6	400°F	200°C
Mark 7	425°F	220°C
Mark 8	450°F	230°C

Please be aware that individual oven performance varies tremendously.

Measurements

Both metric and imperial measurements are given for the recipes. Follow one set of measurements, not a mixture of both, as they are not interchangeable.

Useful-sized Baking Tins and Other Handy Bits and Pieces

Here are the sizes of baking tins used in this book. Heavier, better-quality baking tins conduct heat more efficiently than anything thin and flimsy and have a longer life.

Large baking tray
A baking tray that just fits comfortably inside your oven can be used for scones and the cheese biscuits and oatcakes.

Standard 20cm (8in) square brownie tin
This is a really useful size and shape for brownies and small tray bakes.

12-cup tart tin
It's useful to have two of these for tarts and little pies.

12-cup muffin tin
As well as muffins, this is ideal for buns, fairy cakes and deep-filled pastries.

Pair of 12-cup mini-muffin tins
These are perfect for tiny versions of the above.

Loose-bottomed cake and sandwich tins
It's useful to have the following sizes:

18cm (7in) cake tin
Pair of 18cm (7in) sandwich tins
20cm (8in) cake tin

Loaf tin
450g (1lb) loaf tin

Cooling racks

A cooling rack is a must for cooling your cakes, scones and biscuits and preventing soggy bottoms. If you don't have one, you can use a clean grill rack instead.

Flexible rubber or plastic spatulas

These are extremely useful for scraping the last drop from mixing bowls and for scraping the mixture down from the sides of your food processor bowl.

Lemon reamer

A simple wooden lemon reamer is a quick and easy way to juice a small number of citrus fruits, although in an emergency a dinner fork can work surprisingly well.

Lemon zester

A lemon zester is the best tool for zesting a small amount of citrus fruit.

Large and small palette knives

A small palette knife is useful for removing anything baked directly on a baking tray and for loosening cakes and pastries from baking tins. It's also good for spreading frosting over larger cakes and tray bakes. A large palette knife doesn't have quite so many uses but it's difficult to loosen cakes from the bottom of a loose-bottomed cake tin properly without one.

Tea strainer

A tea strainer is useful for sieving small amounts of lemon juice; or, used with a teaspoon, it's great for dusting ground xylitol over your cakes.

Food processor

Just an ordinary food processor, the kind with the chopping blade that whizzes round, makes beautiful cake mixes. It will also whip up light shortcrust pastry in a twinkling.

Icing bag or syringe

A simple icing bag or syringe with a small selection of piping nozzles is useful for topping or filling your cakes with professionally piped frostings.

Baking with Xylitol

Xylitol can be used in the same way as regular sugar and comes in granulated form. Xylitol works perfectly for most baking but there are a couple of areas where it isn't suitable.

Since it inhibits the growth of yeast it doesn't work for yeast-based baking.

It doesn't caramelise either, so, for example, you couldn't top a crème caramel with it. Your cakes will be golden brown when they come out of the oven, though, as the other ingredients will still brown nicely.

The best xylitol is still made from birch bark, although some brands are now made from corn husks. Try to buy xylitol made from birch bark if you can, it really is of superior quality.

Look for brands such as Total Sweet, which is easily available: you should be able to find it in the sugar section of your local shop.

Tips for Converting Cake Recipes to Xylitol

You may like to try converting other cake recipes that use sugar to xylitol. This is very straightforward for certain types of cake but for others it may not be ideal. Xylitol is as sweet, weight for weight, as regular sugar so you can use the same weight of xylitol as you would sugar. Xylitol comes in pure white, granulated form so is not suitable for rich, dark fruit cakes and sticky gingerbreads. It does, however, make wonderful sponge cakes.

You may find that cakes made with xylitol take a fraction – 2–5 minutes on average – longer to bake than those made with sucrose or regular sugar.

Making your xylitol more like caster sugar for light sponges

Although you can use xylitol, just as it comes, for all the recipes in this book, you may find that for some of the lighter sponge cakes, such as sponge sandwiches and fairy cakes, and pastry, you get even better results if you give the xylitol a few turns in a food processor or grinder before using, to make it a little finer.

Fairies Love Dairy

The Tooth Fairy wholeheartedly approves of milk and dairy products: calcium helps to build strong bones and teeth and milk products help to neutralise the effect of the acids produced by the bugs in your mouth. However, as with all things, moderation is the key: so eat all food groups in balance.

Fruit Spread: a note of caution from the Tooth Fairy

Fruit spread – the kind made only with fruit and possibly a little extra fruit juice, such as apple or grape – contains fruit sugar or fructose. Although the Tooth Fairy prefers this to jam, fructose is still harmful to teeth, unlike xylitol, but *slightly* less so. You could say it is the lesser of two evils – or, as the fairies are fond of saying, the lesser of two weevils!

CHAPTER 1

Fairy Special Selection

Why are the Tooth Fairy's cakes so light and fluffy?

The Tooth Fairy uses plain flour mixed with cream of tartar and bicarbonate of soda (usually at a ratio of 2:1) for extra light cakes. They are sometimes referred to in the method section of each recipe as the 'raising agents'.

The Tooth Fairy also finds the standard type of food processor (the kind that has a blade that whizzes round) an absolute blessing when mixing her cakes; she finds using one results in a perfectly combined and light cake mixture.

This section is full of particular fairy favourites.

Fairy Cakes

175g (6oz) plain flour
1 teaspoon bicarbonate of
soda
2 teaspoons cream of tartar
175g (6oz) butter, softened
175g (6oz) xylitol
3 fresh eggs
2 tablespoons milk

You will need 2 x 12-cup
muffin tins or tart tins (if
you only have one, you will
need to bake a second part
batch) plus standard-size
paper cake cases

Preheat the oven to 180°C
(fan ovens) or equivalent

It's hard to say whether the Tooth Fairy's firmest favourite is fairy cakes or butterfly cakes.

These fairy cakes can be baked in either a muffin tin or a tart tin. The paper cake cases are standard size, however, rather than the more generously proportioned muffin cases.

The Tooth Fairy isn't very keen on a lot of sticky icing on top of her cakes – which is probably just as well, as making glacé icing with xylitol can be tricky. She prefers a light dusting of finely ground xylitol or a little dab of flavoured butter. She is also very partial to **Coconut Frostings** and **Mascarpone Toppings** (see **Toothsome Toppings** on page 20 for recipes for all the frostings and flavoured butters).

1. Add the raising agents to the weighed flour.

2. Whizz the butter and xylitol together in a food processor until combined and fluffy.

3. Sieve in some of the flour and raising agents and add the eggs; sieve in the rest of the flour over the eggs. Whizz again.

4. Add the milk and whizz until smooth and glossy. (You may need to scrape the mixture down from the sides a couple of times with a flexible spatula.)

5. Arrange the paper cases in the muffin tin and spoon two generous teaspoons of mixture into each case.

6. Bake for around 15 minutes or until risen and pale golden and springy to the touch. A skewer or wooden cocktail stick should come out clean when inserted.

7. Remove from the tins and cool on a wire rack.

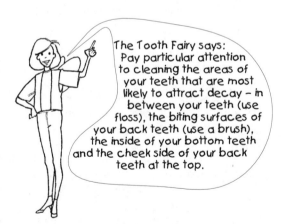

The Tooth Fairy says: Pay particular attention to cleaning the areas of your teeth that are most likely to attract decay – in between your teeth (use floss), the biting surfaces of your back teeth (use a brush), the inside of your bottom teeth and the cheek side of your back teeth at the top.

Teeny Tiny Fairy Cakes

75g (3oz) plain flour
½ teaspoon bicarbonate of
   soda
1 teaspoon cream of tartar
75g (3oz) butter, softened
75g (3oz) xylitol
2 fresh eggs
1 tablespoon milk

You will need 2 x 12-cup
mini-muffin tins plus petit
four paper cases

Preheat the oven to 180°C
(fan ovens) or equivalent

Although this is only half the quantity of mixture of the previous recipe, you certainly seem to end up with a lot of cakes! They are very quick to make and look very cute: just right for your little fairies.

1. Add the raising agents to the weighed flour.

2. Whizz the butter and xylitol together in a food processor until combined and fluffy.

3. Sieve in some of the flour and raising agents and add the eggs; sieve in the rest of the flour over the eggs. Whizz again.

4. Add the milk and whizz until smooth and glossy. (You may need to scrape the mixture down from the sides a couple of times with a flexible spatula.)

5. Arrange the petit four cases in the muffin tins and spoon about a teaspoon of mixture into each case.

6. Bake for around 10 minutes or until risen and pale golden and springy to the touch. A skewer or wooden cocktail stick should come out clean when inserted.

7. Remove from the tins and cool on a wire rack.

Butterfly Cakes

These look so pretty and delicate; the Tooth Fairy always feels very proud when she produces a plate of these.

Make the original fairy cake mix as before and, once the cakes are cool, slice the tops off and put to one side.

Spoon a little dab of **Custard Butter** (page 20) onto each cake and top with a little strawberry, raspberry or apricot fruit spread.

Cut each top in half so you have two 'wings' and arrange on top of each cake.

Just before you want to eat them, sieve some finely ground xylitol over the top as the finishing touch.

If you prefer, you can use the fruit spread on its own without the custard butter.

ASK THE TOOTH FAIRY

How many visits does the tooth fairy make to each child?
Usually 20: one for each milk tooth.

Chocolate Fairy Cakes

150g (5oz) plain flour
1 teaspoon bicarbonate of soda
2 teaspoons cream of tartar
175g (6oz) butter, softened
175g (6oz) xylitol
3 eggs
25g (1oz) good-quality cocoa powder (not drinking chocolate)
2 tablespoons milk

You will need 2 x 12-cup muffin tins or tart tins (if you only have one, you will need to bake a second part batch) plus standard-size paper cake cases

Preheat the oven to 180°C (fan ovens) or equivalent

These are very light and very chocolatey, and always popular.

1. Add the raising agents to the weighed flour.

2. Whizz the butter and xylitol together in a food processor until combined and fluffy.

3. Sieve some of the flour and raising agents in a layer over the mixture and then add the eggs.

4. Sieve in the rest of the flour and the cocoa. Whizz again.

5. Add the milk and whizz until smooth and glossy. You may need to remove the lid a couple of times and scrape the mixture down from the sides with a flexible spatula.

6. Arrange the paper cases in the muffin tin and spoon two fairly generous teaspoons of mixture into each case.

7. Bake for around 15 minutes or until domed and risen and springy to the touch. A skewer or wooden cocktail stick should come out clean when inserted.

8. Remove from the tins and leave to cool on a wire rack.

Chocolate Butterfly Cakes

Make the chocolate fairy cake mix as before and, once the cakes are cool, slice the tops off and put to one side.

Spoon a little dab of **Chocolate Butter** (page 20) onto each cake and top with a little strawberry or raspberry fruit spread.

Cut each top in half so you have two 'wings' and arrange on top of each cake.

Just before you want to eat them, sieve some finely ground xylitol or **Chocolate Dust** (page 23) over the top as the finishing touch.

If you prefer, you can use the fruit spread on its own. The **Custard Butter** (page 20) also works well as an alternative to the **Chocolate Butter**.

The Tooth Fairy says:
Don't rinse your mouth out with water after brushing. It is better to just spit out the froth. You will then leave a thin layer of fluoride over the surface of your teeth to protect them from decay.

Tropical Butterflies

MAKES 12

110g (4oz) plain flour
1 teaspoon bicarbonate of
    soda
2 teaspoons cream of tartar
110g (4oz) butter, softened
110g (4oz) xylitol
2 eggs
2 tablespoons warm water
50g (2oz) desiccated
    coconut

Double quantity of
    Coconut Frosting
    (page 20)

You will need a 12-cup
muffin tin lined with
paper muffin cases

Preheat the oven to 160°C
(fan ovens) or equivalent

These exotic fairy favourites are light and moist
and a little larger than regular butterfly cakes.
For an extra delicious topping, spread a little
raspberry or strawberry fruit spread on top of the
frosting, before positioning the wings.

1. Add the raising agents to the weighed
   flour.

2. Whizz the butter and xylitol together until
   combined and fluffy.

3. Carefully sieve in some of the flour and
   raising agents.

4. Add the eggs and the rest of the flour.

5. Whizz briefly and add the warm water.

6. Whizz until everything is mixed together
   but not over mixed. You may need to stop
   the machine a couple of times and scrape
   the mixture down from the sides.

7. Add the coconut and whizz briefly to mix
   it all in evenly.

8. Using a dessertspoon, divide the mixture
   equally between the 12 muffin cases.

9. Bake for approximately 15–20 minutes,
   until risen and golden and a skewer
   inserted comes out clean.

10. Leave in the tin for a few moments to settle and contract away from the sides.

11. Transfer to a wire rack until completely cold.

12. Once the cakes are cool, slice the tops off and put to one side.

13. Spoon a little dab of **Coconut Frosting** onto each cake.

14. Cut each top in half so you have two 'wings' and arrange on top of each cake.

15. Just before you want to eat them, sieve some finely ground xylitol over the top as the finishing touch.

The Tooth Fairy says:
Flossing is just as important as brushing. Floss your teeth every day.

Chocolate Cup Cakes with Coconut and Vanilla Frosting

Preheat the oven to 160°C (fan ovens) or equivalent

The light chocolate sponge and smooth coconut and vanilla frosting are a magical combination.

Make up the **Chocolate Fairy Cake** (page 6) mixture and line a 12-cup muffin tin with paper muffin cases. Divide the mixture evenly between the 12 muffin cases. Bake for around 18–20 minutes or until domed and risen and a skewer inserted comes out clean.

Make up a double quantity of **Coconut Frosting with Vanilla** (page 21).

Once the cakes are cool, use a piping nozzle suitable for large stars or rosettes on your icing bag or syringe to pipe a generous swirl of frosting onto each cake.

Sprinkle with **Chocolate Dust** (page 23) or desiccated coconut.

Sponge Cake Temperatures and Timings

Suggested temperatures for baking sponge cakes can vary from 160–190°C (fan ovens) or equivalent.

If your oven is a fairly steady average performer, set it to 180°C. If you have a very fierce oven, 160°C may be preferable.

If the finished sponge comes out of the oven flat and hard, it is likely that the temperature was too high and the top cooked before the centre could rise. If the sponge comes out of the oven heavy and not completely cooked, it is likely that the temperature was too low or it wasn't cooked for long enough.

It may be that you will need a couple of attempts at the recipe before you judge matters correctly for your own oven, so the Tooth Fairy advises you to keep notes.

Sponge Cake Sandwiched with Fruit Spread

175g (6oz) plain flour
1 teaspoon bicarbonate of
  soda
2 teaspoons cream of tartar
175g (6oz) butter, softened
175g (6oz) xylitol
3 eggs
2 tablespoons milk

Good-quality fruit spread
Finely ground xylitol, to
  finish

Grease two 18cm (7in)
loose-bottomed sandwich
tins

Preheat the oven to 180°C
(fan ovens) or equivalent
(see 'Sponge Cake
Temperatures and Timings'
on page 11)

Here is the classic teatime sponge cake sandwiched simply with fruit spread. It also works well with a little **Custard Butter** (page 20): spread it over the cake first before the fruit spread. Alternatively, sandwich with **Mascarpone Custard Cream Topping** (page 22).

1. Add the raising agents to the weighed flour.

2. Whizz the butter and xylitol together in a food processor until light and fluffy.

3. Sieve the flour and raising agents in carefully and add the eggs.

4. Whizz again. Add the milk and whizz until the mixture is very smooth and glossy and everything is well mixed. (You may need to scrape the mixture down from the sides a couple of times with a flexible spatula.)

5. Pour into the prepared cake tins using a flexible spatula to help all the mixture out.

6. Bake in the middle of the oven for 18–20 minutes or until the cakes are risen and golden and a skewer inserted comes out clean.

7. Allow the cakes to rest in the tins for a few moments and then carefully loosen the edges with a small palette knife: they should be starting to contract away from the sides of their own accord.

8. If the tins are still too hot to handle, stand the cakes, one at a time, on a jar or something similar. Using both hands, protected with an oven glove or tea towel, pull the side of the tin down so the cake is left, still on its base, on top of the jar. Move it closer to your cooling rack and loosen from the base using a large palette knife. Transfer gently (you may need a fish slice as well as the palette knife at this stage) onto the cooling rack. Repeat with the other cake.

9. Put a small teaspoon of xylitol into a pestle and mortar and grind to a fine powder. Set aside.

10. Once the cakes are cool, spread one with fruit spread; position the other on top, and sieve finely ground xylitol over it.

Fresh Cream Sponge

Fairies love dairy

Whipped fresh cream is a really luxurious filling for a sponge cake. It goes beautifully with either fruit spread or sliced fresh strawberries. Fresh Cream Sponge makes the perfect centrepiece for a special tea.

Make the sponge cake as before and whip **284ml double cream** until thick and spreadable. If you are using **fruit spread**, put that on first and then smooth the cream over the top. If you are using **sliced strawberries**, layer them onto the sponge first, either just as they are or over a thin layer of **strawberry fruit spread**, and smooth the cream carefully over the top.

Cover with the second sponge cake and sieve **finely ground xylitol** over the top.

Fairy Mini Sponge Cakes

You can use the same mix to make around 15 mini sponge cakes. Make the mix as before and bake in two greased 12-cup muffin tins. If you only have one tin, you will need to bake a second part batch. Don't overfill the cups of the muffin tin: the tops of the cakes shouldn't be too domed in appearance.

Leave to settle in the tin for a while and then remove carefully, using a small palette knife to help you.

Cool on a wire rack and, once cool, split and sandwich with raspberry or strawberry fruit spread and dust with finely ground xylitol.

Bake at 160°C (fan ovens) or equivalent for 18–20 minutes or until a skewer inserted comes out clean

ASK THE TOOTH FAIRY

What should you do if the tooth is swallowed by mistake?
Tooth fairies don't mind if there is no tooth to collect because of a genuine accident. A handwritten note under the pillow can be helpful to explain what has happened.

Chocolate Cake

150g (5oz) plain flour
1 teaspoon bicarbonate of
 soda
2 teaspoons cream of tartar
175g (6oz) butter, softened
175g (6oz) xylitol
3 eggs
25g (1oz) good-quality
 cocoa powder (not
 drinking chocolate)
2 tablespoons milk

Plus, fruit spread: raspberry
 seems to go especially
 well with chocolate
Extra xylitol and cocoa to
 finish

Grease two 18cm (7in)
loose-bottomed sandwich
tins

Preheat the oven to 160°C
(fan ovens) or equivalent

You can sandwich this yummy chocolate cake with fruit spread: raspberry or black cherry work well and strawberry and apricot are also good. Alternatively, you can use **Chocolate Butter** (page 20) or one of the **Mascarpone Toppings** (page 22). Finish off with a sprinkling of **Chocolate Dust** (page 23).

1. Add the raising agents to the weighed flour.

2. Whizz the butter and xylitol together in a food processor until combined and fluffy.

3. Sieve some of the flour and raising agents in a layer over the mixture and then add the eggs.

4. Sieve in the rest of the flour and raising agents and the cocoa. Whizz again.

5. Add the milk and whizz until smooth and glossy. (You may need to scrape the mixture down from the sides a couple of times with a flexible spatula.)

6. Pour into the prepared cake tins using a flexible spatula to help all the mixture out.

7. Bake in the middle of the oven for 18–20 minutes until the cakes are risen and a skewer inserted comes out clean.

8. Allow the cakes to rest in the tins for a few moments and then carefully loosen the edges with a small palette knife: they should be starting to contract away from the sides of their own accord.

9. Transfer the cakes gently onto the cooling rack. (See the Sponge Cake recipe on pages 12–13 for more details on removing the cakes from their tins.)

10. Once the cakes are cool, spread one with your chosen filling; position the other on top, and sieve **Chocolate Dust** over it.

Fairy Mini Chocolate Cakes

You can use the same mix to make around 15 mini chocolate cakes. Make the mix as before and bake in two greased 12-cup muffin tins. If you only have one tin, you will need to bake a second part batch. Don't overfill the cups of the muffin tin: the tops of the cakes shouldn't be too domed in appearance.

Leave to settle in the tin for a while and then remove carefully, using a small palette knife to help you.

Cool on a wire rack and, once cool, split and sandwich with raspberry or black cherry fruit spread and dust with **Chocolate Dust**.

Bake at 160°C (fan ovens) or equivalent for 18–20 minutes or until a skewer inserted comes out clean

Fairy Light Brownie

80g (3oz) plain flour
1 teaspoon bicarbonate of
    soda
2 teaspoons cream of tartar
160g (6oz) butter, softened
160g (6oz) xylitol
3 eggs, lightly beaten
25g (1oz) good-quality
    cocoa powder
50g (2oz) ground almonds
2 tablespoons milk

You will need a greased
20cm (8in) square brownie
tin, lined with a piece of
greaseproof paper cut to fit
the bottom (draw round
the bottom of the tin and
cut inside the pencil marks)

Preheat the oven to 180°C
(fan ovens) or equivalent

Not as dense and squidgy as a standard brownie, this is a lighter brownie that is a little less sweet with a lovely deep chocolatey flavour. It's as light as a fairy!

1. Add the raising agents to the weighed flour.

2. Whizz the softened butter and xylitol together until combined and fluffy.

3. Sieve in a little of the flour and raising agents and add the eggs.

4. Add the rest of the flour and raising agents, the cocoa powder, ground almonds and milk.

5. Whizz until smooth, stopping a couple of times to scrape the mixture down from the sides.

6. Remove the blade and scrape into the prepared tin, easing it into the corners.

7. Bake for approximately 25 minutes; depending on your oven it could be a fraction less or a little more. A skewer inserted should *just* show very slight traces of mixture.

8. Mark into squares and cool in the tin. Cover with a clean tea towel to keep the brownies moist. Store in an airtight tin when completely cold.

These are delicious served with **Magic Banana Ice Cream** (page 29).

The Tooth Fairy says: It is better to have a sweet treat which is consumed all in one go and over a fairly short space of time, such as a cake or chocolate bar, rather than a bag of sweets or a lollipop, which represents several short, sharp, sugar attacks, or stays in contact with the teeth for a long time.

Toothsome Toppings

These easy flavoured butters and frostings add an extra little something to your cakes.
Powdered xylitol isn't widely available so you will need to grind some regular xylitol into powder. If you have a small electric grinder, you can start it off in that; otherwise, you will need a pestle and mortar and some elbow grease. If you do use a grinder, finish off in a pestle and mortar for best results.

Custard Butter

50g (2oz) butter, softened
2 teaspoons custard powder
25g (1oz) xylitol, finely ground

Beat the butter until smooth and gradually stir in the sieved custard powder using a wooden or silicon spoon. Once it is all incorporated, stir in the xylitol.

Chocolate Butter

50g (2oz) butter, softened
1 teaspoon cocoa powder
25g (1oz) xylitol, finely ground

Beat the butter until smooth and gradually stir in the sieved cocoa using a wooden or silicon spoon. Once it is all incorporated, stir in the xylitol.

Coconut Frosting

1 x 50g sachet creamed coconut
50g (2oz) butter, softened
25g (1oz) full fat soft cheese
1 heaped teaspoon xylitol, finely ground

The Tooth Fairy is very enthusiastic about this slightly unusual frosting. She approves of the calcium in dairy products (calcium is important for strong, healthy teeth) and likes the way that the oil in the coconut helps the body to absorb calcium.

If you have a mini food processor this is the ideal tool to use, otherwise prepare the frosting in a bowl with a wooden spoon. If you are making a double quantity you can use a standard-sized food processor.

Grate almost all of the creamed coconut, using the coarsest side of your grater, onto a clean board. Set aside.

Whizz or beat the butter until soft and creamy. Whizz or beat in the soft cheese. Add the xylitol and coconut and whizz or beat to mix.

Once you have topped or filled your cake or buns, grate the remaining coconut over the top.

Coconut and Vanilla Frosting

Add a tiny drop or two of good-quality vanilla extract or a small dab of vanilla bean paste to the frosting before you add the coconut and xylitol and mix briefly. You don't need very much: just a little hint of vanilla to complement the coconut rather than overwhelm it.

Coconut Frosting with Lemon, Lime or Orange

Add a little finely grated lemon, lime or orange zest to the frosting with the coconut and xylitol and mix briefly. You don't need very much: just a little hint of citrus to complement the coconut rather than overwhelm it.

250g tub mascarpone
teaspoon (or to taste)
  good-quality vanilla
  extract or vanilla bean
  paste
1–2 teaspoons (or to taste)
  xylitol, finely ground

Mascarpone Topping

Mascarpone makes a dreamy, creamy topping
and goes especially well with chocolate cakes.
A 250g tub of mascarpone provides a
generous amount of topping – you may prefer
to halve the quantities.

Stir the vanilla and ground xylitol into the
mascarpone. If the cake is a chocolate one,
sprinkle a little **Chocolate Dust** over the
mascarpone topping before serving.

250g tub mascarpone
2–3 teaspoons (or to taste)
  custard powder
2 teaspoons (or to taste)
  xylitol, finely ground

Mascarpone Custard Cream Topping

This gorgeous topping is equally delicious
with chocolate or fruit. Serve a little bowl on
the side with any of the **Brownie** recipes or
with the **Banana Tray Bake** or **Strawberry Tray
Bake** or use it to fill a sponge cake. See also
Easy Strawberry Tarts.

Stir the custard powder into the
mascarpone. For best results, stir the custard
powder through a small sieve or tea strainer
with a teaspoon. Stir in the xylitol.

Tooth Fairy Dust

Put a teaspoon of xylitol into a pestle and
mortar and grind until fine. Use to dust over
the top of your cakes. Stirring it through a tea
strainer with a teaspoon gives a nice, even
distribution.

Chocolate Dust

Put about half a teaspoon of xylitol into a pestle and mortar and grind until fine. Stir in a similar amount of cocoa powder and dust over the top of the cake. As before, stirring the cocoa powder through a tea strainer with a teaspoon gives an even distribution. Try this with chocolate cakes and brownies.

Cinnamon Dust

Put about half a teaspoon of xylitol into a pestle and mortar and grind until fine. Stir in a small amount of powdered cinnamon and dust over the top of the cake. Try this with **Carrot Muffins**.

CHAPTER 2

Fruit Fairies

The Tooth Fairy is very fond of fruit and
she enjoys thinking up new ways of
incorporating different types of fruit into
her cakes. She is particularly proud of
her Banana Brownies and Strawberry
Muffins.

Banana Cake

There's something very wholesome about banana cake and the Tooth Fairy is very fond of a slice. The bananas for this recipe need to be just overripe: the skins should be a bit speckled but the banana itself still creamy white.

1. Whizz the butter and xylitol together in a food processor.

2. Add the flours, raising agents, ground almonds and eggs and whizz until combined.

3. Add the banana and whizz that in too.

4. Spoon into the prepared tin, cover loosely with greaseproof paper and bake for about 40–45 minutes, or until a skewer inserted into the cake comes out clean.

5. Loosen the sides and bottom of the cake with a palette knife, remove from tin and cool on a wire rack.

110g (4oz) butter, softened
110g (4oz) xylitol
110g (4oz) wholemeal flour
50g (2oz) plain flour
2 teaspoons cream of tartar
1 teaspoon bicarbonate of soda
50g (2oz) ground almonds
2 fresh eggs
150–175g (5–6oz) ripe bananas (but no more), peeled weight, mashed to a purée but not liquidy

Preheat the oven to 160°C (fan ovens) or equivalent

Grease an 18cm (7in) loose-bottomed cake tin

Banana Muffins

Use the Banana Cake mix to make moreish muffins. The Tooth Fairy finds one of these very sustaining before flying off on a tooth collection.

1. Make up the mixture as for the previous recipe but line the cups of a 12-cup muffin tin with paper muffin cases and divide the mixture equally between them.

2. Bake at 160°C (fan ovens) or equivalent, for approximately 20 minutes, or until a skewer comes out clean.

3. Transfer to a wire rack to cool completely.

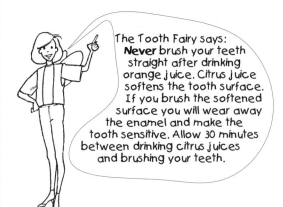

The Tooth Fairy says: **Never** brush your teeth straight after drinking orange juice. Citrus juice softens the tooth surface. If you brush the softened surface you will wear away the enamel and make the tooth sensitive. Allow 30 minutes between drinking citrus juices and brushing your teeth.

Banana Tray Bake

The Banana Cake mix also makes a yummy tray bake. Serve warm, fresh from the oven, or leave to cool.

You will need a greased 20cm (8in) square brownie tin, lined with a piece of greaseproof paper cut to fit the bottom (draw round the bottom of the tin and cut inside the pencil marks)

1. Make up the Banana Cake mix as before.

2. Pour into the prepared tin.

3. Bake at 160°C (fan ovens) or equivalent, for approximately 20 minutes, or until a skewer comes out clean.

4. Leave the cake to settle in the tin for a few minutes and then mark into squares.

5. Transfer to a wire rack to cool completely.

The Tooth Fairy says: Chewing gum increases your saliva flow. If you chew gum after a meal, this will cut down on decay.

Banana Brownie Cake

150g (5oz) plain flour
1 teaspoon bicarbonate of
    soda
2 teaspoons cream of tartar
110g (4oz) butter, softened
175g (6oz) xylitol
3 eggs, lightly beaten
1 teaspoon vanilla extract
25g (1oz) good-quality
    cocoa
    powder
175g (6oz) banana, peeled
    and mashed until
    smooth but not liquidy

You will need a greased
20cm (8in) square brownie
tin lined with a piece of
greaseproof paper cut to fit
the bottom (draw round the
bottom of the tin and cut
inside the pencil marks)

Preheat the oven to 160°C
(fan ovens) or equivalent

Here are two favourite fairy flavours in one: the banana and chocolate complement each other beautifully and the vanilla adds to the enticing taste and aroma.

1. Add the raising agents to the weighed flour.

2. Whizz the softened butter and xylitol together until combined and fluffy.

3. Sieve in a little flour and add the eggs and vanilla.

4. Sieve in the rest of the flour and raising agents and the cocoa and whizz again.

5. Add the banana and whizz until smooth and well mixed. (You may have to stop the machine a couple of times and scrape the mixture down from the sides with a flexible spatula.)

6. Remove the blade from the machine and pour the mixture into the prepared tin, easing it into the corners.

7. Bake for approximately 35–40 minutes until the cake is risen and spongy.

8. Mark into squares and cool in the tin.

9. Cover with a clean tea towel to keep the brownies moist as they cool.

10. Store in an airtight tin when completely cold.

Magic Banana Ice Cream

This is amazing stuff – there is definitely some kind of fairy magic going on here! Make this Magic Banana Ice Cream easily in a food processor, to eat with your Banana Brownie Cake. You will need to freeze the bananas the day before, so allow enough time.

You will need **a couple of ripe bananas**: ripe enough to have a good banana-y flavour but not overripe. The skin can be a bit brown and speckled but the banana itself should still be creamy white.

Peel the bananas and wrap them up snugly in a freezer bag.

Put them into the freezer and leave overnight.

The next day, remove the bananas from the freezer and break them into several pieces.

Whizz in the food processor until smooth. This will take a couple of minutes. At first the banana will look quite stiff and crumbly, but keep going and before long you will have a lovely smooth and creamy banana ice cream. (You may have to scrape the banana down from the sides of the food processor a couple of times with a flexible spatula.)

Eat immediately or put into a lidded freezer box and return to the freezer.

Quick and Easy Orange Buns

80g (3oz) butter, softened
80g (3 oz) xylitol
160g (6oz) plain flour
2 eggs
1 teaspoon bicarbonate of soda
2 teaspoons cream of tartar
Finely grated zest of
   1 orange
2 tablespoons milk

You will need a 12-cup muffin tin, with 10 cups greased: you can't seem to get 10-cup tins!

Preheat the oven to 180°C (fan ovens) or equivalent

These are very quick and easy to make: they also disappear very quickly and easily!

1. Whizz the butter and xylitol together in a food processor until combined and fluffy.

2. Sieve in some of the flour.

3. Add the eggs, the rest of the flour, the raising agents and orange zest. Whizz together.

4. Add the milk and whizz until smooth and glossy.

5. Spoon into the prepared tin, filling each cup about half to three-quarters of the way up.

6. Bake for 12–14 minutes, until risen and pale golden and a skewer inserted comes out clean.

7. Remove from the tin and cool on a wire rack.

8. Store in an airtight container when completely cold.

Eat warm or cold, as they are, or with a little butter.

Quick and Easy Lemon Buns

Lemon zest also works well in these buns. Make in exactly the same way as the previous recipe but add the finely grated zest of one lemon instead of an orange.

The Tooth Fairy says: Children should drink **only water** after brushing their teeth at night. When you go to sleep your saliva flow practically stops, so drinking milk (which is harmless during the day) can rot your teeth at night.

Fairy Light Apple Cake

110g (4oz) butter, softened
110g (4oz) xylitol
175g (6oz) plain flour
1 teaspoon bicarbonate of
    soda
2 teaspoons cream of tartar
50g (2oz) ground almonds
2 eggs
175g (6oz) apple, peeled
    and finely chopped

You will need a greased
18cm (7in) loose-bottomed
cake tin

Preheat the oven to 160°C
(fan ovens) or equivalent

This is a useful recipe: you can eat it cold as a cake or serve it warm as a pudding with a bowl of **Mascarpone Custard Cream Topping** (page 22).

1. Whizz the butter and xylitol together in a food processor.

2. Add the flour, raising agents, ground almonds and eggs and whizz until combined.

3. Add the apple and whizz.

4. Spoon into the prepared tin, cover loosely with greaseproof paper and bake for about 40–45 minutes, or until a skewer inserted into the cake comes out clean.

5. Loosen the sides and bottom of the cake with a palette knife, remove from tin and cool on a wire rack.

Apple Muffins

You can use the Apple Cake mix to make muffins. The Tooth Fairy loves apple cakes at any time of year but really goes to town in the autumn and bakes something apple-y every week. These muffins, and the cinnamon version below, are particular favourites of hers for late weekend breakfasts.

1. Make up the mixture as for the previous recipe but line the cups of a 12-cup muffin tin with paper muffin cases and divide the mixture equally between them.

2. Bake at 160°C (fan ovens) or equivalent, for approximately 20 minutes, or until a skewer comes out clean.

3. Transfer to a wire rack to cool completely.

Apple and Cinnamon Muffins

110g (4oz) butter, softened
110g (4oz) xylitol
175g (6oz) plain flour
1 teaspoon bicarbonate of
  soda
2 teaspoons cream of tartar
50g (2oz) ground almonds
1 teaspoon powdered
  cinnamon
2 eggs
175g (6oz) apple, peeled
  and finely chopped
Plus: an additional 50g
  (2oz) apple, peeled and
  diced

You will need a 12-cup
muffin tin lined with paper
muffin cases

Preheat the oven to 160°C
(fan ovens) or equivalent

This is a similar mix to the previous apple cake recipes but contains cinnamon and small chunks of apple: they smell gorgeous.

1. Whizz the butter and xylitol together in a food processor.

2. Add the flour, raising agents, ground almonds, cinnamon and eggs and whizz until combined.

3. Next, add the 175g (6oz) of chopped apple and whizz.

4. Remove the blade from your processor, scrape any mixture back into the bowl and stir in the 50g (2oz) of diced apple.

5. Spoon into the prepared tin and bake for about 20 minutes, or until a skewer inserted into the buns comes out clean.

6. Remove from the tin and finish cooling on a wire rack.

Apple and Cinnamon Tray Bake

The Apple and Cinnamon Muffin mix works well as a tray bake. Serve warm, fresh from the oven, with **Mascarpone Custard Cream Topping** (page 22), or leave to cool.

1. Make up the Apple and Cinnamon Muffin mix as for the previous recipe.

2. Pour into the prepared tin.

3. Bake for approximately 20–25 minutes until golden, firm to the touch, and a skewer inserted comes out clean.

4. Leave to settle in the tin for a few minutes and then mark into squares.

5. Transfer to a wire rack to cool completely.

You will need a greased 20cm (8in) square brownie tin, lined with a piece of greaseproof paper cut to
fit the bottom (draw round the bottom of the tin and cut inside the pencil marks)

The Tooth Fairy says:
The natural sweetener xylitol has been shown to have a cariostatic effect – it reduces tooth decay – unlike sugar, which leads to decay.

Strawberry Cake

175g (6oz) plain flour
2 teaspoons cream of tartar
1 teaspoon bicarbonate of
  soda
110g (4oz) butter, softened
110g (4oz) xylitol
2 eggs, beaten
A few drops of good-quality
  vanilla extract or a dab
  of vanilla bean paste
50g (2oz) ground almonds
175g (6oz) strawberries,
  sliced

You will need a greased
18cm (7in) loose-bottomed
cake tin

Preheat the oven to 160°C
(fan ovens) or equivalent

This beautiful summery cake is slightly unusual in that strawberries are incorporated into the cake mixture itself.

1. Add the raising agents to the weighed flour.

2. Whizz the butter and xylitol together in a food processor.

3. Sieve half the flour and raising agents over the mixture and add the eggs and vanilla.

4. Add the rest of the flour and the ground almonds. Whizz again.

5. Add the strawberries and whizz until they are all pulped and incorporated into the mixture. (The mixture should now be dusky pink with the odd speck of strawberry.)

6. Spoon into the prepared tin and bake for about 40–45 minutes, or until a skewer inserted into the cake comes out clean.

7. Loosen the sides and bottom of the cake with a palette knife, remove from the tin and cool on a wire rack.

Strawberry Muffins

You can use the Strawberry Cake mix to make muffins. The Tooth Fairy is especially fond of these for breakfast or tea in the garden. She says they are the very taste of summer.

1. Make up the mixture as for the previous recipe but line the cups of a 12-cup muffin tin with paper muffin cases and divide the mixture equally between them.

2. Bake at 160°C (fan ovens) or equivalent, for approximately 20 minutes, or until a skewer inserted comes out clean.

3. Transfer to a wire rack to cool completely.

The Tooth Fairy says: Strictly speaking, it's not how **much** sugar you eat but how **often** you eat sugar which counts. It is much better to eat sweet things all in one go rather than to spread them out over several hours.

Strawberry Tray Bake

You will need a greased 20cm (8in) square brownie tin, lined with a piece of greaseproof paper cut to fit the bottom (draw round the bottom of the tin and cut inside the pencil marks)

The Strawberry Cake mix makes a yummy tray bake. Serve warm, fresh from the oven, or leave to cool.

1. Make up the Strawberry Cake mix as for the above recipe.

2. Pour into the prepared tin.

3. Bake at 160°C (fan ovens) for approximately 25 minutes until golden, firm to the touch, and a skewer inserted comes out clean.

4. Leave to settle in the tin for a few moments and then mark into squares.

5. Transfer to a wire rack to cool completely.

ASK THE TOOTH FAIRY

Should a loose tooth be 'helped out'? Generally, unless the tooth is hanging by a thread and the child is about to go to sleep, the tooth should be left alone to come out in its own good time. Any poking and prodding by the child should definitely be discouraged and may even lead to infection if hands are less than clean.

Light Lemon Loaf

This light little loaf is lovely served just as it is or spread with soft butter. Line your loaf tin with a strip of double thickness greaseproof paper from end to end, with the paper ends sticking up: this will enable you to lift the loaf out easily.

1. Add the raising agents to the weighed flour.

2. Whizz the butter and xylitol together until combined and fluffy.

3. Carefully sieve in some of the flour and raising agents to cover the surface of the butter and xylitol and add the eggs.

4. Add the rest of the flour, the lemon zest and milk.

5. Whizz until everything is smooth and glossy. You may need to stop the machine a couple of times and scrape the mixture down from the sides.

6. Pour the mixture into the prepared tin.

7. Bake for around 45 minutes until risen and golden and a skewer inserted comes out clean.

8. Leave the cake to settle for a few moments and transfer to a cooling rack.

9. Once cold, store in an airtight tin.

175g (6oz) plain flour
1 teaspoon bicarbonate of soda
2 teaspoons cream of tartar
110g (4oz) butter, softened
110g (4oz) xylitol
2 eggs, beaten
Grated zest of 1 lemon
2 tablespoons milk

You will need a greased 450g (1lb) loaf tin lined with a strip of greaseproof paper

Preheat the oven to 160°C (fan ovens) or equivalent

Orange and Almond Cake

2 oranges, not too large: about 150g (5oz) of pulped fruit is ideal
110g (4oz) plain flour
2 teaspoons cream of tartar
1 teaspoon bicarbonate of soda
110g (4oz) butter, softened
110g (4oz) xylitol
110g (4oz) ground almonds
2 eggs, beaten

You will need a greased 18cm (7in) loose-bottomed cake tin

Preheat the oven to 160°C (fan ovens) or equivalent

This cake appeals more to the adult palate. It keeps well in a tin for up to a week, becoming moister and more flavourful.

1. Take one of the oranges and put it, whole and unpeeled, into a pan of cold water. Bring to the boil and simmer, partially covered, for about half to three-quarters of an hour or until it is soft. Cool and cut into several pieces. Remove any pips and central pith, and any bits of membrane that will come away easily. Then put the rest into a food processor and whizz until it is an almost smooth, pale, orange-flecked purée.

2. Peel or grate all the zest from the second orange (a lemon zester works best) and add to the purée. (You will not need the pulp or juice.)

3. Add the raising agents to the weighed flour.

4. Add the butter and xylitol to the purée and whizz until smooth.

5. Add the flour and raising agents, ground almonds and eggs, and whizz until smooth and thoroughly mixed.

6. Pour the mixture into the prepared tin.

7. Bake for about 40–45 minutes, or until golden on top, firm to the touch, and a skewer inserted comes out clean.

8. Cool on a wire rack and eat warm or cold.

Orange and Almond Muffins

You can use the Orange and Almond Cake mix to make muffins: they are lovely at teatime but also wonderful for a relaxed breakfast with a dollop of Greek yoghurt.

1. Make up the mixture as for the previous recipe but line the cups of a 12-cup muffin tin with paper muffin cases and divide the mixture equally between them.

2. Bake at 160°C (fan ovens) or equivalent, for 18–20 minutes, or until a skewer comes out clean.

3. Transfer to a wire rack to cool completely.

Cherry and Almond Cake

100–110g (3½–4oz) dried
  cherries (sometimes
  called dried sour
  cherries)
175g (6oz) plain flour
110g (4oz) butter, softened
110g (4oz) xylitol
2 fresh eggs
1 teaspoon bicarbonate of
  soda
2 teaspoons cream of tartar
4 tablespoons milk
50g (2oz) ground almonds
Approximately 25g (1oz)
  flaked almonds, to
  decorate

You will need a greased
18cm (7in) loose-bottomed
cake tin

Preheat the oven to 160°C
(fan ovens) or equivalent

The Tooth Fairy can be a bit tight-lipped about dried cranberries but she rather likes dried cherries.

This is because, although she admits dried cranberries may contain some valuable vitamins and nutrients, she thinks they are rather acidic and doesn't like the way they are sweetened with sugar. Dried cherries, sometimes called dried sour cherries, however, are usually sweetened with fruit juice, which she feels is a little less harmful.

While the Tooth Fairy wouldn't dream of eating dried cherries as a snack between meals, she is partial to a slice of this cake at teatime, and enjoys the cherries' sweet, yet tart, almost almondy, flavour.

1. Separate the cherries, and cut any that look a bit big in half with kitchen scissors.

2. Take about a tablespoon of flour from the measured amount and toss the cherries in it: although they are dried, they are still moist enough to have a tendency to sink. Set aside until needed.

3. Whizz the butter and xylitol together in the food processor until light and fluffy.

4. Sieve half of the flour over the top and add the eggs.

5. Sieve the rest of the flour, the bicarbonate of soda and cream of tartar over the top and whizz.

6. Add the milk and ground almonds and whizz until everything is fully mixed and smooth.

7. Stop the processor a couple of times and scrape the mixture down from the sides with a flexible spatula.

8. Remove the blade from the food processor and stir in the cherries, distributing them evenly throughout the mixture.

9. Ease the cake mixture into the prepared tin.

10. Scatter the flaked almonds evenly over the top.

11. Bake for about 40–45 minutes until the top is golden and a skewer inserted comes out clean.

12. Transfer to a wire rack and store in an airtight container when completely cold.

Cherry and Almond Muffins

You can use the Cherry and Almond Cake mix to make very moreish muffins.

1. Make up the mixture as for the previous recipe but line the cups of a 12-cup muffin tin with paper muffin cases and divide the mixture equally between them.

2. Bake at 160°C (fan ovens) or equivalent, for approximately 20 minutes, or until a skewer comes out clean.

3. Transfer to a wire rack to cool completely.

Tooth fairies always wear gum shields to protect their front teeth when playing sport.

The Fairies' Vegetable Plot Selection

The Tooth Fairy is a keen gardener and grows quite a large selection of vegetables and herbs. She loves flitting around her plot and choosing something different to put into one of her cakes.

Carrot Cake

110g (4oz) butter, softened
110g (4oz) xylitol
150g (5oz) grated carrot
(grated weight)
Finely grated zest of
1 orange
110g (4oz) wholemeal flour
50g (2oz) plain flour
2 teaspoons cream of tartar
1 teaspoon bicarbonate of
soda
1 teaspoon ground
cinnamon
50g (2oz) ground almonds
2 fresh eggs

You will need an
18cm (7in) greased,
loose-bottomed cake tin

Preheat oven to 160°C
(fan ovens) or equivalent

This delicious carrot cake is full of good wholesome ingredients. Use fresh young carrots for maximum flavour and goodness. Eat it as it is, with a light sprinkling of **Cinnamon Dust** (page 23), or top with **Orange-flavoured Coconut Frosting** (page 21) or **Mascarpone and Vanilla Topping** (page 22).

1. Whizz the butter and xylitol together in a food processor.

2. Add the grated carrot and orange zest and whizz again.

3. Add the flours, raising agents, cinnamon, ground almonds and eggs and whizz until combined.

4. Spoon the mixture into the prepared tin and bake for about 40–45 minutes, or until a skewer inserted into the cake comes out clean.

5. Leave the cake in the tin for a few moments, then loosen the sides and bottom with a palette knife, remove from the tin and cool on a wire rack.

Carrot Muffins

Use the Carrot Cake mix to make moreish muffins. Eat plain or top as suggested for the previous recipe.

1. Make up the mixture as for the previous recipe but line the cups of a 12-cup muffin tin with paper muffin cases and divide the mixture equally between them.

2. Bake at 160°C (fan ovens) or equivalent, for approximately 20 minutes, or until a skewer inserted comes out clean.

3. Transfer to a wire rack to cool completely.

The Tooth Fairy says: Every time you eat something containing sugar, little bugs which live in your mouth produce acid so that they can digest the sugar and enjoy it for themselves. This acid stays in your mouth for about half an hour, dissolving your teeth!

Carrot Tray Bake

You will need a greased 20cm (8in) square brownie tin, lined with a piece of greaseproof paper cut to fit the bottom (draw round the bottom of the tin and cut inside the pencil marks)

The Carrot Cake mix also makes a yummy tray bake. Serve warm, fresh from the oven, or leave to cool.

1. Make up the Carrot Cake mix as before.

2. Pour the mixture into the prepared tin.

3. Bake at 160°C (fan ovens) or equivalent, for approximately 20 minutes, or until a skewer inserted comes out clean.

4. Leave to settle in the tin for a few moments and then mark into squares.

5. Transfer to a wire rack to cool completely.

ASK THE TOOTH FAIRY

Is a special box or bag essential or can you just leave the tooth loose under the pillow?
Tooth fairies don't mind. The main thing to remember is that boxes and bags should be very easy to open. Tooth fairies don't want to be wrestling with anything difficult in the dark when the child could wake at any minute!

Herb Scones

Here's another savoury Tooth Fairy favourite. Eat fresh from the oven with a little butter and possibly some thin slices of cheese.

The Tooth Fairy's own fresh herb combination for these scones is roughly equal quantities of chopped chives, chervil, oregano or marjoram, and a tiny touch of finely chopped thyme.

1. Sieve the flour, bicarbonate of soda and cream of tartar into a bowl large enough to give you room to manoeuvre.

2. Rub in the softened butter.

3. Stir in the xylitol and herbs.

4. Mix in the milk gradually with a dinner knife.

5. Knead gently and place on a floured board.

6. Roll out quite thickly to a depth of about 1cm ($^1/_3$ in), with a floured rolling pin, and cut out with a 6cm (2in) fluted round cutter.

7. Reroll the trimmings and cut out again.

8. Bake on the prepared baking tray for about 10 minutes until the scones are well risen and golden brown on top.

9. Cool on a wire rack.

225g (8oz) plain flour
1 teaspoon bicarbonate of soda
2 teaspoons cream of tartar
40g (1½oz) butter, softened
10g (½oz) unrefined xylitol
About 1 heaped tablespoon of finely chopped garden herbs (or 1 level tablespoon dried mixed herbs)
150ml (¼ pint) semi-skimmed milk, warmed slightly

You will need a greased baking tray

Preheat the oven to 200°C (fan ovens) or equivalent

Sweet Courgette Muffins with Lemon and Vanilla

150g (5oz) courgette,
  peeled and cut into short
  lengths
110g (4oz) butter, softened
110g (4oz) xylitol
Finely grated zest of
  1½ lemons
175g (6oz) plain flour
1 teaspoon bicarbonate of
  soda
2 teaspoons cream of tartar
2 eggs
1 teaspoon good-quality
  vanilla extract
50g (2oz) ground almonds

You will need a 12-cup
muffin tin lined with paper
muffin cases

Preheat the oven to 160°C
(fan oven) or equivalent

The courgette works in a similar way to carrot to add moistness and volume to the cake but has a much more delicate flavour. Cakes made with courgette rise well and have excellent keeping qualities – or so the Tooth Fairy says, anyway!

1. Using the normal blade attachment of your processor, whizz the prepared courgette into strands.

2. Add the butter, xylitol and lemon zest and whizz until combined.

3. Add the raising agents to the flour and sieve half of it over the mixture.

4. Add the eggs and vanilla and sieve in the rest of the flour and raising agents.

5. Whizz briefly and add the ground almonds. Whizz until smooth and well mixed.

6. Divide the mixture between the prepared muffin cups and bake for approximately 20 minutes until risen and golden and a skewer inserted comes out clean.

7. Remove and cool on a wire rack.

8. Cover the muffins with a clean tea towel to keep them moist and prevent them drying out as they cool.

Chocolate and Courgette Brownies

175g (6oz) courgette, peeled and cut into short lengths
110g (4oz) butter, softened
175g (6oz) xylitol
150g (5oz) flour
1 teaspoon bicarbonate of soda
2 teaspoons cream of tartar
3 eggs, lightly beaten
1 teaspoon vanilla extract
25g (1oz) good-quality cocoa powder

You will need a greased 20cm (8in) square brownie tin, lined with a piece of greaseproof paper cut to fit the bottom (draw round the bottom of the tin and cut inside the pencil marks)

Preheat the oven to 160°C (fan ovens) or equivalent.

Chocolate and courgette sounds an unlikely combination but the two work very well together to make a lighter, moister version of the classic brownie. The Tooth Fairy makes these every summer.

1. Using the normal blade attachment of your processor, whizz the prepared courgette into strands.

2. Add the butter and xylitol and whizz until combined.

3. Add the raising agents to the flour and sieve half of it over the mixture.

4. Add the eggs and vanilla and sieve in the rest of the flour and raising agents and the cocoa. Whizz until smooth and well mixed. (You may have to stop the machine a couple of times and scrape the mixture down from the sides with a flexible spatula.)

5. Remove the blade from the machine and pour the mixture into the prepared tin, easing it into the corners.

6. Bake for approximately 30 minutes; depending on your oven it could be a fraction less or a little more. A skewer inserted should just show very slight traces of mixture.

7. Mark into squares and cool in the tin.

8. Cover the brownies with a clean tea towel to keep them moist as they cool.

9. Store in an airtight tin when completely cold.

The Tooth Fairy says: Taking sugar in your tea or coffee means that you are subjecting your teeth to several extra acid attacks every day.

Cheese and Courgette Muffins

MAKES 12

175g (6oz) courgette, peeled and cut into short lengths
110g (4oz) butter, softened
10g (½oz) xylitol
225g (8oz) plain flour
2 teaspoons cream of tartar
1 teaspoon bicarbonate of soda
½ teaspoon mustard powder (or to taste)
A small pinch of salt
2 fresh eggs
75g (3oz) well-flavoured mature Cheddar cheese, grated

You will need a 12-cup muffin tin, greased and lined with paper muffin cases

Preheat the oven to 160°C (fan ovens) or equivalent

The Tooth Fairy was keen to have a few savoury recipes in her book, and this is one of her summertime favourites. Eat as they are or spread with a little soft butter.

1. Using the normal blade attachment of your processor, whizz the prepared courgette into short strands.

2. Add the butter and xylitol and whizz until fluffy.

3. Combine the cream of tartar, bicarbonate of soda, mustard and salt with the flour and sieve half of it over the mixture.

4. Add the eggs.

5. Sieve the rest of the flour, mustard and raising agents over the top and whizz until thoroughly mixed.

6. Add the cheese and whizz briefly: the mixture will remain fairly stiff.

7. Spoon into the prepared tin, dividing the mixture as equally as possible.

8. Bake for about 20 minutes, or until the muffins are springy to the touch and a skewer inserted comes out clean.

9. Remove the muffins from the tin and cool on a wire rack.

10. Cover with a clean tea towel to keep them moist and prevent them drying out as they cool.

CHAPTER 4

Flower Fairies' Selection

The Tooth Fairy loves flowers and always has posies in little jugs and vases arranged on her tea-table. Sometimes she actually bakes the flowers into her cakes to surprise and delight her guests.

Fennel Flower Surprise from the Tooth Fairy

If you have access to some unsprayed fennel flowers in your garden or herb patch, either the decorative bronze fennel (**Foeniculum vulgare** 'purpureum') or the normal green variety (**Foeniculum vulgare**), you can have a surprisingly sweet and aniseedy experience. Each tiny little yellow flower that makes up the umbrella-like flower head tastes like a miniature aniseed ball and explodes in your mouth with flavour.

You can use the flowers as an unusual edible garnish for salads, sandwiches and cakes. Whole flower heads look striking, or pull off the tiny individual flowers and scatter them over the food.

Scented Geranium Cake

110g (4oz) butter, softened
110g (4oz) xylitol
175g (6oz) plain flour
1 teaspoon bicarbonate of
    soda
2 teaspoons cream of tartar
2 eggs
2 tablespoons warm water
Approximately 6 lemon-
    scented geranium leaves

You will need a greased
18cm (7in) round loose-
bottomed cake tin

Preheat the oven to 160°C
(fan ovens) or equivalent

Lemon-scented geranium leaves are used for this recipe but you may like to try rose-scented geranium leaves if you are feeling adventurous.

1. Whizz the butter and xylitol together until combined and fluffy.

2. Carefully sieve in some of the flour.

3. Add the eggs and the rest of the flour and the raising agents. Whizz briefly, and add the warm water.

4. Whizz until everything is mixed together but not over mixed. You may need to stop the machine a couple of times and scrape the mixture down from the sides.

5. Lay the scented geranium leaves over the bottom of the prepared cake tin, pressing them down lightly.

6. Pour the cake mix into the tin, carefully over the leaves: they need to stay flat so you can peel them away after baking.

7. Bake for around 45 minutes, until the cake is risen and golden and a skewer inserted comes out clean.

8. Leave in the tin to settle and contract away from the sides for a few moments then transfer to a wire rack until completely cold.

9. Once the cake is cold, peel the geranium leaves carefully away from the bottom and store it in an airtight tin.

The Tooth Fairy says: Tooth fairies always eat three square meals a day. This means that they don't feel the need to snack between meals.

Marigold Buns

80g (3oz) butter, softened
80g (3oz) xylitol
160g (6oz) plain flour
1 teaspoon bicarbonate of
　soda
2 teaspoons cream of tartar
2 eggs
2 tablespoons milk
Petals from about 8
　unsprayed, bug-free,
　orange pot marigold
　flowers

You will need a 12-cup
muffin tin, with 10 cups
greased: you can't seem to
get 10-cup tins!

Preheat the oven to 180°C
(fan ovens) or equivalent

The Tooth Fairy loves these buns: the marigold flavour doesn't come through very strongly but, if you concentrate hard, there is a very subtle, almost aniseed flavour. Eat warm or cold, as they are, or with a little butter.

The marigolds used in this recipe are the English pot marigold, **Calendula officinalis** (not the much more pungent French or African marigold, **Tagetes**).

To separate the petals from the flowers
Hold each flower in one hand and gather the petals together in the other. Give a sharp tug and they will all come away from the centre together.

1.　Whizz the butter and xylitol together in a food processor until combined and fluffy.

2.　Sieve in some of the flour and add the eggs.

3.　Sieve in the rest of the flour and the raising agents. Whizz again.

4.　Add the milk and whizz until smooth and glossy.

5. Remove the blade from the machine and stir in the marigold petals.

6. Spoon into the prepared tin, filling each cup about half to three-quarters of the way up.

7. Bake for 12–14 minutes, until the buns are risen and pale golden and a skewer inserted comes out clean.

8. Remove from the tin and cool on a wire rack.

9. Store in an airtight container when completely cold.

The Tooth Fairy says:
Fairies Floss First!
Floss **before** you brush –
that way you open up the
spaces between your teeth
so that the toothpaste can
get in and protect the
contact areas.

Rose Cup Cakes with Coconut and Rose Frosting

MAKES 12

For the cakes
175g (6oz) butter, softened
175g (6oz) xylitol
175g (6oz) plain flour
1 teaspoon bicarbonate of soda
2 teaspoons cream of tartar
3 fresh eggs
2 tablespoons milk
A few tiny drops of culinary rose water

For the topping
Double quantity of Coconut Frosting
A couple of drops of culinary rose water or rose essence
Crystallised rose petals to decorate
Fresh rose petals, to dress serving plate

You will need a 12-cup muffin tin plus muffin-size paper cake cases

Preheat the oven to 160°C (fan ovens) or equivalent

These cakes are very pretty to look at and lovely and light to eat. Success depends entirely on **not going overboard with the rose flavouring** – just a very little hint of rose is sufficient. Otherwise, you may feel as though you are eating a bath bomb! You can make the serving plate look gorgeous with a scattering of fresh rose petals and put fresh roses on the table.

1. Whizz the butter and xylitol together in a food processor until combined and fluffy.

2. Sieve in some of the flour, the bicarbonate of soda and cream of tartar and add the eggs; sieve in the rest of the flour over the eggs. Whizz again.

3. Add the milk and whizz until smooth and glossy. (You may need to scrape the mixture down from the sides a couple of times with a flexible spatula.) Stir in the rose water.

4. Arrange the paper cases in the muffin tin and, using a dessertspoon, divide the mixture equally between them.

5. Bake for around 18 minutes or until risen and pale golden and springy to the touch. A skewer or wooden cocktail stick should come out clean when inserted.

6. Remove from the tin with a small palette knife and cool on a wire rack.

7. Once the cakes are cool, stir a couple of drops of rose water or rose essence into the coconut frosting.

8. Spoon a dollop of the frosting onto the top of each cake for a casual, countrified look; or, for something more formal, use a piping bag to pipe a generous swirl of frosting on top. (Use a piping nozzle suitable for large stars or rosettes on your icing bag or syringe.)

9. Decorate the cakes with crystallised rose petals and garnish the serving plate with fresh rose petals.

Lavender Scones

225g (8oz) plain flour
1 teaspoon bicarbonate of soda
2 teaspoons cream of tartar
40g (1½oz) butter, softened
10g (½oz) xylitol
About 5–10 spikes of lavender flowers, no more
150ml (¼ pint) semi-skimmed milk, warmed slightly

You will need a greased baking tray

Preheat the oven to 200°C (fan ovens) or equivalent

The Tooth Fairy always chooses lavender that is still in bud and deep purple, as, once the flowers open, they can feel a bit 'bristly' in the mouth. As with the previous recipe for **Rose Cup Cakes**, it's important not to overdo the lavender flavour or your scones will be too overpoweringly scented to enjoy.

A word of warning: be sure to use only the more common English lavender, **Lavandula angustifolia**, sometimes called **Lavandula officinalis** or **Lavandula spicata**. The tufty French lavender, **Lavandula stoechas**, can be toxic.

1. Lay the lavender spikes on kitchen paper for a while to dry out and allow any minibeasts to leave. Remove all the florets from the stalks and shake them lightly in a sieve.

2. Sieve the flour, bicarbonate of soda and cream of tartar into a bowl large enough to give you room to manoeuvre.

3. Rub in the softened butter.

4. Stir in the xylitol and lavender.

5. Mix in the milk gradually, using an ordinary dinner knife.

6. Knead gently and place on a floured board.

7. Roll out quite thickly with a floured rolling pin to a depth of around 1½cm (³/₄) ins.

8. Cut out with a 6cm (2in) fluted cutter.

9. Re-roll the trimmings and cut out again.

10. Bake on the prepared baking tray for 8–10 minutes until the scones are well risen and golden brown on top.

11. Cool on a wire rack.

Eat warm or cold, with butter or clotted cream and fruit spread.

The Tooth Fairy says:
Children should normally
start flossing
as soon as their premolar
teeth come through at
around 12 or 13 years old.

CHAPTER 5

Traditional Cake Selection

The Tooth Fairy enjoys baking all the traditional old favourites and likes to have something classic to offer when older fairies fly over to visit.

Chocolate and Almond Cake

You can eat this lovely moist and chocolatey cake just as it is or split and filled with fruit spread: raspberry or black cherry both work beautifully. You can also sieve a little **Chocolate Dust** (page 23) over the top as the finishing touch.

1. Whizz the butter and xylitol together in the food processor until light and fluffy.

2. Add the raising agents to the flour and sieve half of it over the mixture.

3. Add the eggs and sieve the rest of the flour, raising agents and the cocoa over the top and whizz.

4. Add the milk and ground almonds and whizz until everything is fully mixed and smooth.

5. Stop the processor a couple of times and scrape the mixture down from the sides with a flexible spatula.

6. Ease the cake mixture into the prepared tin.

7. Bake for about 40–45 minutes until the top is firm yet springy to the touch and a skewer inserted comes out clean.

8. Transfer to a wire rack and store in an airtight container when completely cold.

110g (4oz) butter, softened
110g (4oz) xylitol
150g (5oz) plain flour
1 teaspoon bicarbonate of soda
2 teaspoons cream of tartar
2 fresh eggs
25g (1oz) good-quality cocoa powder (not drinking chocolate)
4 tablespoons milk
50g (2oz) ground almonds

You will need a greased 18cm (7in) loose-bottomed cake tin

Preheat the oven to 160°C (fan ovens) or equivalent

Madeira Cake

175g (6oz) plain flour
1 teaspoon bicarbonate of
  soda
2 teaspoons cream of tartar
110g (4oz) butter, softened
110g (4oz) xylitol
2 eggs
Grated zest of 1 lemon
  (optional)
2 tablespoons warm water

You will need a greased
18cm (7in) round loose-
bottomed cake tin

Preheat the oven to 160°C
(fan ovens) or equivalent

Here is a lovely old-fashioned cake, plain and not at all fancy. The lemon zest gives a fresh taste to the cake but, if you prefer, you can leave it out. The Tooth Fairy always makes this when her godmother comes to tea.

1. Add the raising agents to the weighed flour.

2. Whizz the butter and xylitol together until combined and fluffy.

3. Carefully sieve in some of the flour and raising agents.

4. Add the eggs, the rest of the flour and the lemon zest, if using. Whizz briefly and add the warm water.

5. Whizz until everything is mixed together but not over mixed. You may need to stop the machine a couple of times and scrape the mixture down from the sides.

6. Pour the mixture into the prepared tin and cover loosely with greaseproof paper, tucking it under the tin to secure. You need to have the tension of the paper just right so that it protects the cake from drying out without dipping down onto the surface and sticking to it.

7. Bake for 45–50 minutes, until the cake is risen and golden and a skewer inserted comes out clean.

8. Leave in the tin for a few moments to settle and contract away from the sides, then transfer to a wire rack until completely cold. Once cold, store in an airtight tin.

Custard Butter Buns

The combination of the Madeira sponge and the custard and fruit spread is irresistible. The Tooth Fairy loves these: the custard flavour reminds her of happy lunchtimes with her young fairy friends years ago at Fairy School.

Make the **Madeira Cake** mix as before. Divide the mixture between the cups of the prepared tin.

Bake at 160°C (fan ovens) or equivalent for 18–20 minutes or until a skewer inserted comes out clean.

Leave to settle in the tin for a while and then remove carefully, using a small palette knife to help you.

Cool on a wire rack and, once cool, split the buns and sandwich with softened **Custard Butter** (page 20) and **strawberry or raspberry fruit spread**.

You will need a greased 12-cup muffin tin

Seed Cake

175g (6oz) plain flour
1 teaspoon bicarbonate of
soda
2 teaspoons cream of tartar
110g (4oz) butter, softened
110g (4oz) xylitol
2 eggs
2 tablespoons warm water
2 teaspoons caraway seeds

You will need a greased
18cm (7in) round loose-
bottomed cake tin

Preheat the oven to 160°C
(fan ovens) or equivalent

Here is another old-fashioned cake recipe: perfect for a traditional afternoon tea. The caraway seeds give the cake the most beautiful flavour.

1. Add the raising agents to the weighed flour.

2. Whizz the butter and xylitol together until combined and fluffy.

3. Carefully sieve in some of the flour and raising agents.

4. Add the eggs and the rest of the flour and raising agents.

5. Whizz briefly and add the warm water.

6. Whizz until everything is mixed together but not over mixed. You may need to stop the machine a couple of times and scrape the mixture down from the sides.

7. Remove the blade from the machine and stir in the caraway seeds.

8. Pour the mixture into the prepared tin and cover loosely with greaseproof paper, tucking it under the tin to secure. You need to have the tension of the paper just right so that it protects the cake from scorching without dipping down onto the surface and sticking to it.

9. Bake for 45–50 minutes until risen and golden and a skewer inserted comes out clean.

10. Leave in the tin for a few moments to settle and contract away from the sides, then transfer the cake to a wire rack until completely cold.

11. Once cold, store in an airtight tin.

Caraway Muffins

Make the mixture as for the **Seed Cake** recipe above and line a 12-cup muffin tin with paper muffin cases. Using a dessertspoon, divide the mixture equally between the 12 cups. Bake at 160°C, as before, for approximately 12–15 minutes until risen and golden and a skewer inserted comes out clean.

Cool on a wire rack. Once completely cold, store the muffins in an airtight container.

Light Fruit Cake

110g (4oz) butter
110g (4oz) xylitol
200ml (scant 7 fl oz) water
225g (8oz) dried fruit:
   currants, raisins and
   plenty of sultanas
225g (8oz) plain flour
1 teaspoon bicarbonate of
   soda
2 teaspoons cream of tartar
2 fresh eggs, lightly beaten

You will need a greased
18cm (7in) loose-bottomed
cake tin

Preheat the oven to 160°C
(fan ovens) or equivalent

This is a light, traditional-style fruit cake. It's very easy to put together and the Tooth Fairy sometimes bakes one of these when her grandmother pays one of her flying visits.

1. Cut the butter into small pieces and put into a saucepan with the xylitol, water and fruit.

2. Bring to the boil and simmer for five minutes, stirring from time to time.

3. Leave to cool.

4. Add the raising agents to the flour and sieve half of it over the mixture.

5. Add the eggs and sieve the rest of the flour and raising agents over the top.

6. Mix everything together thoroughly with a wooden spoon.

7. Spoon the mixture into the prepared tin, making sure the fruit is evenly distributed throughout. (If you pour it into the baking tin too quickly, you can be left with plain mixture in the saucepan at the end, which will mean your cake has a layer of fruit-free mixture on the top!)

8. Wrap the tin loosely in greaseproof paper, tucking it underneath to secure: the tension needs to be just right so that the cake is covered but the paper doesn't dip down into the mixture as it rises.

9. Bake for about 65–75 minutes or until the cake is golden in colour and a skewer inserted comes out clean.

10. Cool on a wire rack and store in an airtight tin.

Light Fruit and Spice Cake

Sometimes, when her grandmother visits, especially on cooler days, the Tooth Fairy likes to mix it up a little and add a touch of warming spice to her grandmother's favourite cake. Make the mixture as for the **Light Fruit Cake** but add a teaspoon of mixed spice and a teaspoon of powdered cinnamon with the butter and dried fruit. Proceed as for the main recipe.

Cherry, Chocolate and Almond Muffins

100–110g (3½–4oz) dried cherries (sometimes called dried sour cherries)
150g (5oz) plain flour
110g (4oz) butter, softened
110g (4oz) xylitol
1 teaspoon bicarbonate of soda
2 teaspoons cream of tartar
2 fresh eggs
25g (1oz) good-quality cocoa powder (not drinking chocolate)
4 tablespoons milk
50g (2oz) ground almonds

You will need a 12-cup muffin tin lined with paper muffin cases

Preheat the oven to 160°C (fan ovens) or equivalent

These are delicious just as they are but fabulous with a dollop of **Mascarpone Topping** (page 22) and a sprinkling of **Chocolate Dust** (page 23).

1. Separate the cherries, and cut any that look a bit big in half with kitchen scissors.

2. Take about a tablespoon of flour from the weighed amount and toss the cherries in it. Set aside until needed.

3. Whizz the butter and xylitol together in the food processor until light and fluffy.

4. Add the raising agents to the flour and sieve half of it over the mixture.

5. Add the eggs and sieve the rest of the flour, raising agents and the cocoa over the top and whizz.

6. Add the milk and ground almonds and whizz until everything is fully mixed and smooth.

7. Stop the processor a couple of times and scrape the mixture down from the sides with a flexible spatula.

8. Remove the blade from the food processor and stir in the cherries, distributing them evenly throughout the mixture.

9. Using a dessertspoon, divide the mixture equally between the muffin cases.

10. Bake for about 18–20 minutes until the muffins are firm yet springy to the touch and a skewer inserted comes out clean.

11. Transfer to a wire rack and store in an airtight container when completely cold.

The Tooth Fairy says:
If you have orange or grapefruit juice with your breakfast it is better to brush your teeth **before** breakfast.

Deep-filled Mini Tarts

160g (6oz) plain flour
A pinch of salt
80g (3oz) cold butter,
   diced
1 tablespoon xylitol
3 tablespoons cold water

Fruit spread for filling

You will need 2 x 12-cup
greased mini-muffin tins
and a 6cm (2½in) fluted
or plain cutter

Preheat the oven to 180°C
(fan ovens) or equivalent

These dainty little tarts are a firm fairy favourite.
Fill with strawberry, raspberry, apricot or
blackcurrant fruit spread: it's quite nice to use
two or three flavours so you can offer a mixed
plate of tarts.

1. Sieve the flour and salt carefully into the
   bowl of your food processor and add the
   butter. Whizz into fine crumbs.

2. Add the xylitol and whizz again briefly.

3. Add the water and whizz until the mixture
   is starting to come together.

4. Turn the mixture out onto a floured
   board and knead it lightly until it forms a
   ball.

5. Roll it out gently with a floured rolling
   pin to a thickness of just less than ½cm
   (¼in).

6. Cut out 24 circles with the cutter, transfer
   them to the prepared tins and firm them
   down gently.

7. Fill each tart with no more than a
   teaspoon of fruit spread: they need to be
   generously filled but not so much that as
   the filling heats up it boils out of the tarts.

8. Bake for 10–12 minutes until the pastry is lightly golden.

9. Keep the tart tins level as you take them out of the oven: if you tilt them the practically molten fruit filling can spill out of the tarts at this stage.

10. Remove the tarts from the tin with a small palette knife when they are cool enough to handle and finish cooling on a wire rack.

The Tooth Fairy says: 'Take care! Never eat a tart fresh from the oven when the filling is still boiling hot!'

The Tooth Fairy says:
If you want to consume sugar it is better to have it at mealtimes, when there is more saliva in your mouth to wash it away.

Mini Apple Pies

For the pastry
160g (6oz) plain flour
A pinch of salt
80g (3oz) cold butter,
    diced
1 tablespoon xylitol
3 tablespoons cold water

For the filling
10g (½oz) butter
10g (½oz) xylitol
2–3 dessert apples,
    peeled and cored,
    approximately 200g
    (7oz) prepared weight
A generous 10g (½oz)
    sultanas
 teaspoon cinnamon
    (optional)

You will need 2 fluted
cutters: 1 x 7½cm (3in)
and 1 x 6cm (2½in) and
a greased 12-cup tart tin

Preheat the oven to 180°C
(fan ovens) or equivalent

Handy and portable, these little pies are perfect for picnics. If you aren't fond of sultanas, leave them out; similarly, leave the cinnamon out if you prefer.

1. Sieve the flour and salt carefully into the bowl of your food processor and add the butter. Whizz into fine crumbs.

2. Add the xylitol and whizz again briefly.

3. Add the water and whizz until the mixture is starting to come together.

4. Turn the mixture out onto a floured board and knead it lightly until it forms a ball.

5. Roll it out gently with a floured rolling pin to a thickness of just less than ½cm (¼in).

6. Cut out 12 circles with the larger cutter (for the pies) and 12 circles with the smaller cutter (for the lids).

7. Put the larger circles into the prepared tart tins and firm them down gently.

8. Set the smaller circles aside while you make the filling.

9. Melt the butter and add the xylitol and the cinnamon (if using) once the butter is starting to soften. Cut the apple into small chunks and stir into the melted butter with the sultanas until all the pieces are coated.

10. Put a lid on the pan and cook gently until the apple is just starting to soften and the sultanas are starting to plump up.

11. Divide the apple filling equally between the pastry cases.

12. Brush the edges of the tarts with water and put the lids on.

13. Press each lid down very, very gently.

14. Make a little hole or slit in the top of each lid.

15. Bake for 12–15 minutes until the pastry is lightly golden.

16. Remove the pies from the tin with a small palette knife, when cool enough to handle, and finish cooling on a wire rack.

Easy Strawberry Tarts

160g (6oz) plain flour
A pinch of salt
80g (3oz) cold butter, diced
1 tablespoon xylitol
3 tablespoons cold water

Plus **Mascarpone Custard Cream Topping** (page 22) to fill
Sliced fresh strawberries

You will need a 12-cup muffin tin with 10 cups greased and a 10cm (4in) fluted or round cutter.
Plus baking beans (preferably ceramic) and greaseproof paper

Preheat the oven to 180°C (fan ovens) or equivalent

The only slight fiddle with these is lining the pastry cases, but apart from that it's all very straightforward.

1. Cut out 10 circles of greaseproof paper to fit the bottoms of the muffin cups and put your baking beans into a jug with a good pouring spout for ease of use.

2. Sieve the flour and salt carefully into the bowl of your food processor and add the butter. Whizz into fine crumbs.

3. Add the xylitol. Whizz again briefly.

4. Add the water and whizz until the mixture is just starting to come together.

5. Turn the mixture out onto a floured board and knead it lightly until it forms a ball.

6. Roll it out gently on a very lightly floured board with a lightly floured rolling pin to a thickness of just less than ½cm (¼in).

7. Cut out the pastry rounds and, using the tips of the first two fingers of each hand, press them gently into the prepared muffin tin. Put a little circle of greaseproof paper in each one and fill almost to the brim with baking beans.

8. Bake for 15 minutes or until the pastry is crisp and golden.

9. Leave to settle and cool slightly in the tin.

10. Remove the baking beans and greaseproof paper.

11. Once cool, fill with a couple of teaspoons of **Mascarpone Custard Cream Topping** (page 22) and smooth the tops with the back of the spoon.

12. Ease the tarts carefully out of the tin with a small palette knife.

13. Before serving, arrange the sliced strawberries over the tops.

ASK THE TOOTH FAIRY

Do tooth fairies always come at night?
Not necessarily. Some actually prefer to slip in during the day when children are at school.

Coconut Cake

110g (4oz) butter, softened
110g (4oz) xylitol
110g (4oz) plain flour
2 eggs
1 teaspoon bicarbonate of
soda
2 teaspoons cream of tartar
2 tablespoons warm water
50g (2oz) desiccated
coconut

You will need a greased
18cm (7in) round loose-
bottomed cake tin

Preheat the oven to 160°C
(fan ovens) or equivalent

This is a lovely moist coconut cake. As has been said before, the Tooth Fairy approves wholeheartedly of coconut: the oil in the coconut helps the body absorb calcium, which as we know helps build strong teeth.

1. Whizz the butter and xylitol together until combined and fluffy.

2. Carefully sieve in some of the flour.

3. Add the eggs and the rest of the flour and the raising agents.

4. Whizz briefly and add the warm water.

5. Whizz until everything is mixed together but not over mixed. You may need to stop the machine a couple of times and scrape the mixture down from the sides.

6. Add the coconut and whizz briefly to mix it all in evenly.

7. Pour the mixture into the prepared tin and cover loosely with greaseproof paper, tucking it under the tin to secure. You need to have the tension of the paper just right so that it protects the cake from scorching without dipping down onto the surface and sticking to it.

8. Bake for approximately 40–45 minutes, until the cake is risen and golden and a skewer inserted comes out clean.

9. Leave in the tin for a few moments to settle and contract away from the sides.

10. Transfer to a wire rack until completely cold.

11. Once cold, store in an airtight tin.

Coconut Muffins

Make the mixture as for the **Coconut Cake** recipe above and line a 12-cup muffin tin with paper muffin cases.

Using a dessertspoon, divide the mixture equally between the 12 cups. Bake at 160°C, as before, for approximately 18–20 minutes, until risen and golden and a skewer inserted comes out clean.

Cool on a wire rack. Once completely cold, store the muffins in an airtight container.

Coconut and Raspberry Buns

Make the mixture as for the **Coconut Cake** recipe as before and grease a 12-cup muffin tin.

Using a dessertspoon, divide the mixture equally between the 12 cups. Bake at 160°C, as before, for approximately 12–15 minutes, until risen and golden and a skewer inserted comes out clean.

Leave to settle in the tin for a few minutes – they are very fragile at this stage. Then lever them out very gently, using a small palette knife, and transfer to a wire rack to finish cooling.

Once completely cold, split the buns horizontally and spread with raspberry fruit spread.

Before serving, put a small teaspoonful of xylitol in a pestle and mortar and grind to a fine powder. Dust over the buns.

Store the buns in an airtight container.

Plain Scones, Sandwiches and Cheesy Savoury Favourites

Here is a selection of sandwiches, scones and cheesy savouries to complement your cakes.

Plain Scones

225g (8oz) plain flour
1 teaspoon bicarbonate of
  soda
2 teaspoons cream of tartar
40g (1½oz) butter,
  softened
10g (½oz) xylitol
150ml (¼ pint) semi-
  skimmed milk, warmed
  slightly

You will need a greased
baking tray

Preheat the oven to 200°C
(fan ovens) or equivalent

Scones don't need to be too sweet: 10g of xylitol is just right. These are perfect with strawberry fruit spread, a dollop of clotted cream and a few strawberries on the side. The Tooth Fairy likes to 'huddle' her scones together on the baking tray: she says it's cosier that way. They certainly turn out well, baked like this with softer sides where they have been pushed up against their neighbours.

You can also try these scones with a little **Custard Butter** and some fruit spread.

Scones should really be eaten as fresh as possible but if you have any left over, they are very good split and very lightly toasted under the grill the next day.

1. Sieve the flour, bicarbonate of soda and cream of tartar into a bowl large enough to give you room to manoeuvre.

2. Rub in the softened butter.

3. Stir in the xylitol.

4. Mix in the milk gradually using an ordinary dinner knife.

5. Knead gently and place on a floured board.

6. Roll out quite thickly – a generous 2cm ($^3/_4$ in) – with a floured rolling pin, and cut out with a 6cm (2½ in) cutter (a fluted one looks professional).

7. Reroll the trimmings and cut out again, although these won't be quite as good as the ones you cut out first.

8. Place the scones together on the prepared baking tray so that they are touching each other.

9. Bake for 8–10 minutes, until well risen and golden brown on top.

10. Cool on a wire rack, covered with a clean tea towel to keep them moist as they cool.

The Tooth Fairy says:
Tooth fairies don't drink fizzy drinks often but when they do they always use a straw. This means that the fizzy drink doesn't come into contact with their front teeth. Fizzy drinks are made by adding carbon dioxide and either flavouring or fruit juice to water. Carbon dioxide and water makes carbonic acid. This is how fizzy drinks harm your teeth.

Cream Cheese and Nasturtium Sandwiches

Nasturtium leaves and flowers, and the flower buds, are surprisingly good to eat and a firm favourite with the fairies. They taste very like mustard cress and look gorgeous with their glowing jewel-like colours.

They make a beautiful dainty little sandwich: use **brown bread** and spread with just a little **butter** and some **cream cheese**.

You need **4–6 unsprayed youngish nasturtium leaves, completely bug free,** per round of sandwiches. Fold each leaf in half, cut along the fold, and then roll it up and snip over the cream cheese once you have spread it over the bread.

When you have made your sandwiches, cut the crusts off and cut into dainty triangles. Serve garnished with more leaves and some of the flowers. (The Tooth Fairy likes to put some flowers and flower buds in the sandwiches as well.)

Cucumber and Borage Sandwiches

Borage flowers (and the very small, young, non-bristly borage leaves) taste faintly of cucumber and are edible. If you have any in your garden, you can use them to make an unusual cucumber sandwich.

Pick some **borage flowers** by pulling them gently away from the plant by their black centres. Lay them on some kitchen paper and set aside, making sure they are completely bug free.

Peel a section of **cucumber** and cut it into wafer thin slices. Lay the slices on a double thickness of kitchen paper and sprinkle lightly with salt. Lay a couple more layers of kitchen paper on top and leave for a while. This draws out excess moisture from the cucumber and concentrates the flavour.

Spread some slices of **fresh bread** (thin slices for teatime, or chunkier ones for a quick lunchtime snack) with softened **butter**. Make a sandwich of the sliced cucumber topped with a scattering of borage flowers.

If the sandwiches are for teatime, remove the crusts, cut into dainty triangles and garnish with another scattering of borage flowers.

Borage flowers are also called 'star flowers' and are said to promote cheerfulness. The Tooth Fairy loves them and she's certainly always very cheerful!

'Toothbrush' Sandwiches with Cheese, Celery and Sesame Seeds

Ever since the Tooth Fairy read that cheese, celery and sesame seeds have a cleaning action on your teeth as you eat them, she has been very keen on these sandwiches.

Spread some slices of **fresh brown bread** (thin slices for teatime, or chunkier ones for a quick lunchtime snack) with softened **butter**. Make into sandwiches with thinly sliced or grated **Cheddar cheese**, thinly sliced **celery** and a light scattering of **sesame seeds**.

The Tooth Fairy likes to serve these sandwiches with some sticks of carrot and cucumber on the side: she says they have a cleaning action on teeth as well.

Cheese Party Shapes

The Tooth Fairy likes to cut non-crumbly cheeses such as mild Cheddar, Edam or Gouda into ½cm (¼in) slices and cut out simple shapes with fancy cutters. She arranges them on a separate plate on the tea table for birthday parties and encourages her guests to eat one at the end of the meal. Sometimes she slips them into lunch boxes.

The Tooth Fairy whizzes up the leftover cheese trimmings in the food processor to make a rather bumpy grated cheese and stores it in a bag in the freezer. She finds it handy for cooking as there is no need to defrost.

The Tooth Fairy says: You probably know that tooth fairies never, ever, smoke. Apart from all the other health issues, they know that smoking reduces the blood supply to the gums, increasing the risk of gum disease, which is a major cause of tooth loss.

Custard Butter Sandwiches

Make some sandwiches with thinly sliced, very fresh bread. Spread the bread with some softened **Custard Butter** (page 20) and then a layer of **fruit spread: strawberry, raspberry or apricot** all work well. Remove the crusts and cut into dainty triangles.

Chocolate Butter Sandwiches

Make some sandwiches with thinly sliced, very fresh bread. Spread the bread with some softened **Chocolate Butter** (page 20). Cut off the crusts and cut into dainty triangles: quick, simple and a real treat.

Open-faced Strawberry Sandwiches

During the summer, when strawberries are plentiful, you can make a simple teatime treat with **a slice of fairly thickly cut very fresh bread** spread with **clotted cream** and sliced fresh **strawberries**: preferably warm from the garden.

You can also make a delicious open-faced strawberry sandwich by spreading the bread with **Chocolate Butter** or **Custard Butter** (page 20) instead of clotted cream and topping with the strawberries.

Sometimes, during the winter, the Tooth Fairy makes these sandwiches with sliced banana instead of strawberries.

The Tooth Fairy says:
Fizzy water in itself does not harm your teeth – but the flavouring that's added to clear, flavoured fizzy water is extremely acidic and will make your teeth very sensitive.

Cheese Scones

225g (8oz) plain flour
1 teaspoon bicarbonate of
soda
2 teaspoons cream of tartar
A generous pinch of
mustard powder
40g (1½oz) butter,
softened
10g (½oz) xylitol
75g (3oz) well-flavoured
Cheddar cheese, mature
if possible, grated
150ml (¼ pint) semi-
skimmed milk, warmed
slightly

You will need a greased
baking tray

Preheat the oven to 200°C
(fan ovens) or equivalent

For a stronger cheese flavour, use the same amount of cheese as in the recipe, but choose a mature vintage variety. If you add extra cheese instead, the texture of the finished scones can be affected and they may well have a slightly heavy and greasy feel to them.

Eat these warm from the oven with a little butter.

1. Sieve the flour, bicarbonate of soda, cream of tartar and mustard powder into a bowl large enough to give you room to manoeuvre.

2. Rub in the softened butter.

3. Stir in the xylitol and cheese.

4. Mix in the milk gradually using a dinner knife.

5. Knead gently and place on a floured board.

6. Roll out to a depth of 2cm (³/₄in) with a floured rolling pin.

7. Cut out with a 6cm (2½in) fluted round cutter.

8. Reroll the trimmings and cut out again, although these won't be quite as good as the ones you cut out first.

9. Bake on the prepared baking tray for 8–10 minutes until the scones are well risen and golden brown on top.

10. Cool on a wire rack.

ASK THE TOOTH FAIRY

Why is the money the tooth fairy leaves behind so bright and shiny?
Tooth fairies use brand new money, fresh from the mint. Apparently, you can make dull coins almost as shiny as fairy gold by soaking them in white spirit vinegar (distilled vinegar) and then buffing them up with a silver polishing cloth. Rinse and pat dry.

The Tooth Fairy sometimes makes her coins extra shiny by polishing them with the inside of a ripe banana skin. She has also been known to buff up her godmother's silver tea service in the same way.

Is it true that the tooth fairies leave extra money if the tooth comes out on Christmas Day?
This is the case in some areas. Some tooth fairies leave as much as double the usual amount and may do the same if the tooth comes out on the child's birthday!

Light Cheesy Buns

110g (4oz) butter, softened
10g (½oz) xylitol
225g (8oz) plain flour
2 teaspoons cream of tartar
1 teaspoon bicarbonate of
soda
A good pinch of mustard
powder – around
½ teaspoon
A small pinch of salt
2 fresh eggs
4 tablespoons milk
75g (3oz) well-flavoured
mature Cheddar cheese

You will need a greased
12-cup muffin tin and
12 muffin-size paper cake
cases

Preheat the oven to 160°C
(fan ovens) or equivalent

These light and fluffy, savoury fairy favourites are very child-friendly. Eat them fresh from the oven, just as they are, or cold with a little soft butter.

1. Whizz the butter and xylitol together in a food processor.

2. Add the raising agents, mustard powder and salt to the weighed flour. Carefully sieve in half of this and then add the eggs.

3. Sieve the rest of the flour, mustard and raising agents over the top and whizz briefly.

4. Add the milk and whizz again.

5. Add the cheese. Whizz until combined: the mixture will remain fairly stiff.

6. Spoon into the prepared tin, dividing the mixture as equally as possible.

7. Bake for about 15 minutes, or until the buns are springy to the touch and a skewer inserted comes out clean.

8. Leave in the tin for a few minutes, as they are very fragile at this stage, and then ease them out gently with a small palette knife.

9. Cool on a wire rack. Cover with a clean tea towel to keep them moist and prevent them drying out as they cool.

Wicked Cheese and Chilli Muffins from the Fire Fairies

Cheese and chilli always go well together. These appeal more to the adult palate. Make the muffins as above and add **half a teaspoon or so of chilli powder** to the dry ingredients at the beginning and proceed as for the main recipe.

Alternatively, fry **fresh red chilli** (amount to taste) in **a small amount of oil**, drain briefly on kitchen paper and add with the cheese. One advantage of using fresh chillies is that they show up attractively in the finished buns. Again, proceed as for the main recipe.

The Tooth Fairy says: Finishing a meal with cheese will help to neutralise the effect of the acids produced by the bugs in your mouth.

Cheesy Biscuits

50g (2oz) plain flour
A pinch of dry mustard
    powder
A pinch of salt
25g (1oz) butter, softened
75–110g (3–4oz)
    well-flavoured Cheddar
    cheese, grated

You will need a large
greased baking tray and
some biscuit cutters

Preheat the oven to 180°C
(fan ovens) or equivalent

You can use plain or fancy cutters for these savoury biscuits. The Tooth Fairy usually has a plate of these to offer at all her parties and get-togethers.

The lesser amount of cheese will make a slightly less rich biscuit, the greater amount will be a little cheesier and richer.

1. Sieve the flour and mustard powder carefully into the bowl of your food processor, sprinkle in the salt and add the butter.

2. Give the mixture a quick whizz to start everything off and add the cheese.

3. Keep whizzing, stopping from time to time to remove the lid and give the mixture a quick stir, until the mixture starts to clump together.

4. Stop the machine, remove the blade and transfer the mixture to a clean board.

5. Gently bring the mixture together with your hands and knead it lightly until it looks and feels like a ball of cheesy marzipan.

6. Flour the board lightly and, using a floured rolling pin, roll out to a thickness of just less than 1cm (½in).

7. Cut out your shapes and arrange on the prepared tray.

8. Re-roll the trimmings and cut out the rest.

9. If you have any dough left over, roll it into little balls and flatten with your hand or a fork and bake with the others.

10. Bake for 7–8 minutes, or until the biscuits are golden in colour.

11. Remove from the oven and leave to settle for a few moments.

12. Carefully remove the biscuits from the tray with a palette knife and finish cooling on a wire rack.

13. Store in an airtight tin.

The Tooth Fairy says: Dried fruit is not a healthy alternative to sweets: although in many ways it is more nutritious than sweets, tooth fairies aren't very keen on dried fruit between meals. Each little fruit is packed full of concentrated fruit sugar (fructose) which can be harmful to teeth. Not only is dried fruit full of sugar, it is also very sticky so it gets stuck in the tiny grooves on the surface of your teeth, causing decay. It's not a good choice as a snack: it's better eaten at mealtimes rather than in between meals.

Easy Oatcakes

225g (8oz) medium oatmeal, plus quite a bit more for rolling
75ml (3 fl oz) *warm* water (cold water doesn't bring the mixture together properly and it will be too crumbly to work with)
A pinch of salt, if liked

You will need a large greased baking tray and a plain, round (not fluted) 7cm (3in) cutter

Preheat the oven to 200°C (fan ovens) or equivalent

The Tooth Fairy likes to make these when she has plenty of time: she can't seem to keep the mixture together if she's distracted and in a rush. She likes working with oatmeal: she says it helps keep her hands soft.

The ingredients are very simple: just oatmeal and warm water with a touch of salt. Eat the oatcakes with butter and cheese or fruit spread. They will keep for several days in an airtight container.

1. Put the oatmeal into a roomy bowl and mix in the warm water with a wooden spoon. If you are using salt, dissolve it in the water first.

2. Spread some more oatmeal onto your board or work surface and rub some onto your hands (it will all fall off but you will be left with a faint powdery coating).

3. Shape the mixture in the bowl into a ball, gathering up any loose crumbs, and pour a little more oatmeal over it.

4. Lift it onto the board and, making sure it is completely coated in oatmeal, roll it to about the thickness of a pound coin.

5. Keep your rolling pin dusted with oatmeal and free from sticky crumbs throughout.

6. Cut into rounds using a plain, round (not fluted) 7½cm (3in) cutter, and transfer to the greased baking tray.

7. Bake for around 15 minutes, until the oatcakes are crisp but not coloured, turning them over after 7 or 8 minutes.

8. Cool on a wire rack.

If you are left with a lot of oaty crumbs at the end, put them back in the bowl and remoisten with a drop more warm water, then you can reroll the ball.

If you become a dab hand at these and make them regularly, you might like to use a small cutter to make some fairy-sized mini oatcakes: much appreciated by children and good for entertaining.

 **ASK THE TOOTH FAIRY**

And finally . . .What do the tooth fairies do with all those teeth?
Traditionally, female tooth fairies would fly to collect the teeth, while male fairies ground up the teeth to make fine china, for fairy tea sets – much like bone china but more delicate. They also make keys for fairy pianos, buttons and other bits and pieces, and tiny shapes for games similar to chess, draughts and dominoes – except that the pieces are all white! These days both sexes can be found doing either task.

Magic Cheese Spread

Fairies love dairy

110g (4oz) Cheddar cheese
1 tablespoon semi-skimmed milk
3–4 teaspoons rapeseed oil (or similar mild oil)

Use a food processor to magic up this delicious spread from a chunk of cheese and a splash or two of milk and oil. Eat on buttered toast or crumpets or use to make sandwiches and top rolls or plain biscuits. During the summer, a few snipped chives scattered over the spread in a sandwich or on a roll work well.

There is no need for extra seasoning: the flavour of the cheese speaks for itself.

1. Cut the cheese into smaller pieces and whizz in the processor until it becomes rather bumpy grated cheese.

2. Add the milk and whizz briefly.

3. Add a teaspoon of oil and whizz again.

4. Add the rest of the oil and whizz until smooth: you may need to stop the processor a couple of times and scrape the cheese down from the sides with a flexible spatula.

Index